"Discover Exclusive Deals: Your Ultimate Affiliate Shopping Guide" is a strong and enticing title for an affiliate marketing advertisement. It conveys a sense of exclusivity and value to potential customers, making them curious to explore your affiliate offers. It implies that your guide will help them find unique and money-saving deals, making it a great choice for attracting shoppers interested in discounts and savings.

Click here Affiliate Marketing Make Money $100/DAY

- Unlock Savings: Affiliate Marketing Magic Just for You!" is a catchy and engaging title for an affiliate marketing advertisement. It creates a sense of intrigue and personalization, suggesting that the viewer can access special savings tailored to their needs. The word "magic" adds a touch of excitement and wonder, making it more likely to grab the attention of potential customers who are looking for discounts and deals. This title should appeal to those seeking unique and cost-effective shopping opportunities.
-
-
-
-

"Shop Smart and Save Big with Our Top Affiliate Picks" is a compelling title for an affiliate marketing advertisement. It communicates the idea that by using the recommended affiliate products or services, customers can make informed choices and enjoy significant savings. This title should attract shoppers who want to make wise purchasing decisions while getting the best value for their money. It's a great choice for affiliate marketing campaigns promoting quality and cost-effective options.

"Secret Discounts Revealed: Affiliate Marketing Favorites" is an enticing title for an affiliate marketing advertisement. It suggests that the viewer is about to uncover exclusive and hidden discounts by exploring your recommended affiliate products. The use of "favorites" implies that these are trusted and highly-regarded choices. This title can pique the interest of bargain-hunting customers who are looking for savings and deals they might not find elsewhere

"Maximize Your Savings: Affiliate Marketing Specials Await" is an effective title for an affiliate marketing advertisement. It conveys a clear message that viewers have an opportunity to increase their savings by taking advantage of affiliate marketing specials. The word "await" adds a sense of anticipation and urgency, encouraging potential customers to take action. This title should appeal to those seeking ways to get the most value out of their purchases.

"Get More for Less: Explore Affiliate Marketing Wonders" is an engaging and persuasive title for an affiliate marketing advertisement. It implies that viewers can access exceptional value through affiliate marketing, which is likely to attract those looking for quality products or services at a lower cost. The word "wonders" adds an element of curiosity and excitement, making it even more compelling. This title effectively conveys the idea that customers can benefit from affiliate marketing offers.

Affiliate All-Stars: Best Products, Best Prices" is a strong and straightforward title for an affiliate marketing advertisement. It suggests that the products or services you're promoting through affiliate marketing are top-notch, and customers can get them at the best prices. The term "All-Stars" adds a sense of excellence and reliability to the offerings, making it a compelling choice for those seeking quality and affordability. This title is likely to resonate with shoppers looking for the best deals on the market.

"Your Money, Your Way: Affiliate Marketing Power" is a persuasive and empowering title for an affiliate marketing advertisement. It implies that customers have control over their spending and can leverage the power of affiliate marketing to make decisions that align with their preferences. The title suggests that affiliate marketing gives consumers the ability to save money and make choices that suit their needs. This can be appealing to individuals seeking a personalized and cost-effective shopping experience.

"Don't Pay Full Price! Find Discounts Through Affiliate Marketing" is a direct and effective title for an affiliate marketing advertisement. It clearly communicates the value proposition to potential customers, emphasizing the opportunity to save money by utilizing affiliate marketing offers. This title should resonate with budget-conscious shoppers and those looking for ways to cut costs while making their purchases. It's a compelling and actionable message that can drive interest and engagement.

"Shop Smarter, Not Harder: Affiliate Marketing for Savvy Shoppers" is a clever and appealing title for an affiliate marketing advertisement. It encourages viewers to be more strategic in their shopping, suggesting that affiliate marketing is the key to doing so. The term "savvy shoppers" implies that this approach is for those who want to make informed and cost-effective choices. This title should attract individuals looking to optimize their shopping experience and get the best value for their money.

"The Ultimate Shopping Experience: Affiliate Marketing Bonanza" is an enticing title for an affiliate marketing advertisement. It portrays affiliate marketing as a grand and exciting shopping adventure, inviting viewers to explore and benefit from the variety of offers available. The word "bonanza" suggests an abundance of deals and discounts, making it appealing to shoppers seeking a wide range of options and savings. This title can generate interest and encourage viewers to take part in the affiliate marketing experience.

"Affiliate Magic: Where Savings and Quality Meet" is a captivating and imaginative title for an affiliate marketing advertisement. It creates a sense of enchantment and suggests that affiliate marketing is the place where cost-effective shopping and high-quality products converge. This title is likely to attract shoppers looking for both savings and quality, making it a compelling choice for an affiliate marketing campaign.

"Shop with Confidence: Affiliate Marketing Goldmine" is a reassuring and attractive title for an affiliate marketing advertisement. It conveys the idea that affiliate marketing offers a reliable and profitable shopping experience. The term "goldmine" suggests that viewers can discover valuable deals and savings, making it a strong choice for those seeking confidence in their purchasing decisions. This title is likely to resonate with shoppers looking for trustworthy and lucrative opportunities.

"Save, Shop, Repeat: Mastering Affiliate Marketing" is a catchy and informative title for an affiliate marketing advertisement. It implies a continuous cycle of savings, shopping, and learning to master the art of affiliate marketing. This title should attract individuals looking for a sustainable way to save money while making purchases. It suggests that viewers can achieve expertise in the field, making it an appealing choice for those seeking long-term value and savings.

"Affiliate Deals Galore: Your Gateway to Savings" is a compelling title for an affiliate marketing advertisement. It suggests that there are numerous deals and discounts available through affiliate marketing, making it an attractive choice for price-conscious shoppers. The term "gateway" implies that viewers can access these savings easily and conveniently. This title is likely to resonate with those looking for a wide array of money-saving opportunities.

Affiliate marketing is a performance-based online marketing strategy where individuals or businesses (affiliates) promote products or services from another company (the merchant) and earn a commission for each sale or action generated through their marketing efforts. Here's a summary of affiliate marketing education:

Understanding Affiliate Marketing:

Affiliate marketing involves three main parties: the affiliate, the merchant, and the consumer.
Affiliates promote products or services through various online channels like websites, social media, email, or content marketing.

Choosing a Niche:

Affiliates should select a niche or
industry they are passionate about
and have expertise in, as it helps with
content creation and audience
engagement.
Joining Affiliate Programs:

Affiliates need to sign up for affiliate
programs offered by merchants.
These programs provide tracking links
and marketing materials.
Creating Content:

Affiliates often create content to
promote the products or services,
such as blog posts, reviews, videos, or
social media posts.

SEO and Content Optimization:

Understanding search engine optimization (SEO) is crucial for improving content visibility in search results, which can drive organic traffic.
Building an Audience:

Building and nurturing an engaged audience is essential. This can be done through social media, email lists, and other channels.

Tracking and Analytics:

Monitoring affiliate marketing performance is crucial. Most programs provide analytics to track clicks, conversions, and commissions earned. Compliance and Disclosure:

Affiliates should adhere to ethical standards by disclosing their affiliate relationships to their audience. Compliance with regulations is essential.

Experimentation and
Optimization:

Successful affiliate marketers
often experiment with
different strategies and
continually optimize their
campaigns for better results.
Monetization Methods:

Affiliates earn commissions
through various methods,
including pay-per-sale, pay-
per-click, pay-per-lead, or
hybrid models

Choosing Affiliate Products and Services:

It's important to select products or services that align with the affiliate's niche and target audience.
Networking and Building Relationships:

Building relationships with merchants and other affiliates can lead to valuable insights, collaborations, and promotional opportunities.

Long-Term Strategy:

Sustainable success in affiliate marketing often requires a long-term approach, focusing on audience growth and trust.
Adaptation and Staying Informed:

The digital marketing landscape is continually evolving, so staying updated on industry trends and technology is crucial for sustained success.

Legal and Tax Considerations:

Understanding tax implications and legal requirements related to affiliate marketing income is essential.
In summary, affiliate marketing involves promoting products or services from a merchant, earning commissions for successful referrals. Success in affiliate marketing requires a combination of marketing skills, content creation, audience building, and continuous optimization. It's a versatile way to generate income online, but it requires dedication and ongoing learning to stay competitive in the digital marketing space.

Overall, affiliate marketing is a powerful online business model that can provide individuals and businesses with the opportunity to generate revenue and expand their online presence. However, it's not a get-rich-quick scheme; success requires dedication, the right strategies, and ongoing education. When executed effectively, affiliate marketing can be a mutually beneficial arrangement for all parties involved.